Experiments
with
LIGHT

Isabel Thomas

raintree

a Capstone company — publishers for children

Raintree is an imprint of Capstone Global Library Limited, a company incorporated in England and Wales having its registered office at 7 Pilgrim Street, London, EC4V 6LB – Registered company number: 6695582

www.raintree.co.uk
myorders@raintree.co.uk

Edited by Clare Lewis and Amanda Robbins
Designed by Steve Mead
Picture research by Eric Gohl
Production by Victoria Fitzgerald
Originated by Capstone Global Library Ltd
Printed and bound by CTPS in China

ISBN 978 1 406 29031 8
18 17 16 15 14
10 9 8 7 6 5 4 3 2 1

British Library Cataloguing in Publication Data
A full catalogue record for this book is available from the British Library.

Acknowledgements
We would like to thank the following for permission to reproduce photographs: iStockphotos: Kali Nine LLC, 6; Shutterstock: Basileus, 11, charnsitr, 7 (top), Marcel Clemens, 16 (bottom), Ozerov Alexander, 7 (bottom), Piotr Krzeslak, 10, raysay, 23 (bottom)

All other photographs were created at Capstone Studio by Karon Dubke.

We would like to thank Patrick O'Mahony for his invaluable help in the preparation of this book.

Every effort has been made to contact copyright holders of material reproduced in this book. Any omissions will be rectified in subsequent printings if notice is given to the publisher.

All the Internet addresses (URLs) given in this book were valid at the time of going to press. However, due to the dynamic nature of the Internet, some addresses may have changed, or sites may have changed or ceased to exist since publication. While the author and publisher regret any inconvenience this may cause readers, no responsibility for any such changes can be accepted by either the author or the publisher.

Safety instructions for adult helper
The experiments in this book should be planned and carried out with adult supervision. Certain steps should only be carried out by an adult – these are indicated in the text. Always follow the instructions carefully, and take extra care when using scissors (p18 and p24), mirrors (p22 and p24) and electrical devices such as torches (p8, p12, p18, p22 and p24). Never look at the Sun directly. The publisher and author disclaim, to the maximum extent possible, all liability for any accidents, injuries or losses that may occur as a result of the information or instructions in this book.

Contents

Some words are shown in bold, **like this**. You can find out what they mean by looking in the glossary.

Why experiment?

What makes objects different colours? How do shadows form? Why can't we see ourselves in a mirror if we look at it from the side? You can answer all these questions by investigating light.

Scientists ask questions like these. They work out the answers with the help of **experiments**.

Get your eyes ready! You'll need to observe your experiments carefully and record what you see.

An experiment is a test that has been carefully planned to help answer a question.

The experiments in this book will help you to understand what light is and how it behaves. You'll learn how to work like a scientist, and have lots of fun along the way!

IS IT A FAIR TEST?

Most experiments involve changing something to see what happens. Make sure you only change one thing, or **variable**, at a time. Then you will know that it was the variable you changed that made the difference. This is called a fair test.

WARNING! Ask an adult to help you plan and carry out each experiment. Follow the instructions carefully. Look out for this sign.

ADULT HELP

Follow these steps to work like a scientist.

Ask a question.

Come up with an idea to test.

Plan an experiment.

What will you change?
What will you keep the same?
What will you measure?

Make a **prediction**.

Observe carefully.

Work out what the results mean.

Answer the question!

What is light?

Light is a form of **energy**. Our eyes detect light energy. This allows us to see all the objects and colours around us.

Where does light come from?

Many light objects are hot objects. Stars, flames and electric lamps all give off light. As the light travels away, it transfers energy from the **light source** to its surroundings.

REAL WORLD SCIENCE

The Sun is Earth's nearest star, and our brightest light source. Energy from the Sun travels to Earth as light. As well as allowing us to see, it keeps the planet warm and helps plants to grow. We couldn't live without light.

The Moon looks bright, but it is not a light source. We can see the Moon because light from the Sun bounces off it and travels to our eyes.

Never look at the Sun directly, or through any kind of binoculars or telescope. You could damage your eyes forever and even go blind.

Light is produced in other ways too. This **bioluminescent** jellyfish gives off light because of **chemical changes** inside its body.

We see light sources because the light they give off travels to our eyes. Most objects are not light sources. We only see them when light bounces off them towards our eyes.

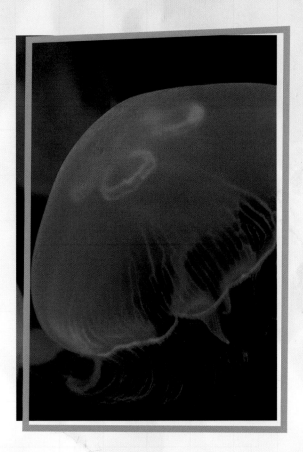

SEE THE SCIENCE ⤵

The light from a lamp or the Sun looks colourless or white but it is actually made up of seven different colours. When light is split into these colours we see a rainbow. Try splitting light by shining a beam of white light through a glass or a jug of water.

Sources of light

Is every bright or shiny object a **light source**?
This **experiment** will help you to find out.

EQUIPMENT

- Cardboard box with tightly fitting lid
- Pencil
- Torch
- Small plastic toy
- Bright and shiny objects to test

Method

1 Put the toy spider in the box and close the lid. Carefully use the pencil to make a small hole in the side of the box.

2 Put your eye to the hole. What can you see?

Predict: Will you be able to see the spider if you put the light source in the box?

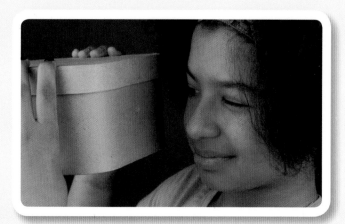

3 Now turn the torch on and put it inside the box with the spider. Replace the lid and look through the hole. Can you see the torch? Can you see the spider?

Predict: Which other objects are light sources?

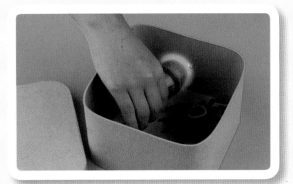 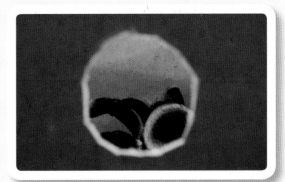

4 Try out the other objects you have collected, one at a time. Draw a table to record your predictions and **observations**.

Object	Prediction: Will you be able to see the object in the closed box?	Observations: Can you see the object?
Torch		
Mirror		
Bike reflector		
LED		
Digital clock display		

5 **Analyse** your results. Which objects are light sources?

Conclusion

When you put a light source inside the box, light from the source also bounces off other things in the box and allows you to see them. Not every bright object is a light source though. Without light, we cannot see.

How does light travel?

Light travels amazingly fast. The sunlight hitting Earth now has travelled 150 million kilometres (92 million miles) since it left the Sun eight minutes ago!

Most of light's journey from the Sun to Earth is through space, which is a **vacuum**. Light travels at about 300,000 kilometres (186,000 miles) per second in a vacuum. Light can also travel through other substances, such as air, but more slowly.

Light can pass through some materials, such as clear glass. We say these "see-through" materials are **transparent**.

In air, light travels about a million times faster than sound. This is why we see the lightning flash before we hear the sound it makes.

Other materials, such as wood and metal, stop light from passing through them. These materials are **opaque**.

Translucent materials, such as tissue paper, let some light through. These materials scatter the light, so shapes look fuzzy.

opaque

transparent

translucent

Different materials allow different amounts of light to pass through them.

SEE THE SCIENCE ⬇

When light travels from air into a liquid or solid, it slows down. This causes it to change direction. Try shining a narrow beam of light through a jug of jelly. What happens to the light as it slows down? The light rays speed up again as they move from the jelly back into air.

Glowing lanterns

To make these glowing lanterns, you need a **translucent** material that will let some light through, but hide the **light source** inside. This **experiment** will help you to find the best material for your own spooky lantern.

EQUIPMENT

* Torch
* Box
* Range of different materials to test, such as card, writing paper, tracing paper, acetate, tissue paper, foil, plastic wrap, crepe paper, different fabrics or foam packaging
* Pencil
* Scissors

Method

1 Set up a torch in a box so it points upwards. Darken the room if you can. Can you see how the beam of light passes through the air and hits the ceiling?

2 Cut a square of your first material and use it to cover the torch. Look up at the ceiling. Can the light from the torch pass through the material? Record what you see. Is the paper **transparent**, translucent or **opaque**?

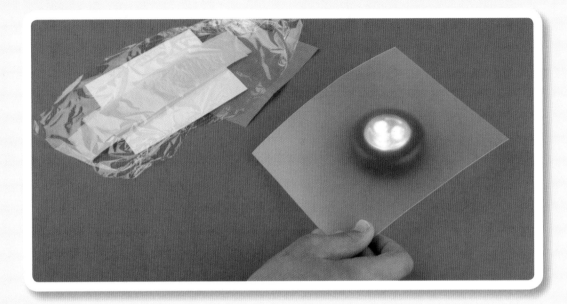

3 Add another layer of the same material. What happens? Record the number of sheets you have to add to block the light from the torch completely.

4 Repeat steps 2 and 3 using different materials and record what happens.

 IS IT A FAIR TEST?

You should only change the material itself. Everything else should stay the same. Is it a fair test if each material is a different thickness? How could you improve your experiment?

5 Draw a table to record your results. This will make it easier to compare them.

Material	How much light does it let through? All, some or none?	How many layers before light blocked out?
None	All	
Paper		
Foil		

6 **Analyse** your results. Which materials are **opaque**? Which are **transparent**? Which are **translucent**? Which ones would be best for making a glowing paper lantern?

7 Draw a pattern on one side of a small box or paper bag. Ask an adult to help you cut it out. Stick a sheet of your chosen translucent material inside the box or bag, so it covers the cut-out pattern. Put a **light source** inside the lantern and watch it come to life!

Light your lanterns with a glow stick, torch or battery-powered tea light.

Conclusion

Transparent materials let most light pass through them. We can see through them. Translucent objects let some light pass through them. We can't see through them. Opaque objects don't let any light pass through them. Translucent materials are best for making a glowing lantern. As you add more layers, translucent materials become less translucent.

What are shadows?

Light travels in a straight line. When it hits an **opaque** object, light can't pass through the object or bend around it. No light reaches the other side. A dark area called a shadow is formed.

A shadow is the same shape as the object blocking the light.

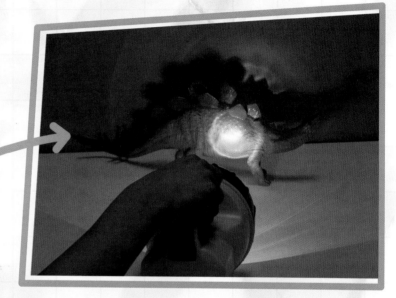

Light cannot pass through the dinosaur so a shadow forms.

REAL WORLD SCIENCE

Half of the Earth is always in shadow. The edge of the shadow is called the terminator. It's the line between day and night.

terminator

Your body casts a shadow when it blocks the path of light from the Sun, and stops the sunlight from hitting the ground.

As the Sun's position in the sky changes, the size and position of your shadow changes too. The higher the Sun is overhead, the shorter your shadow. It is shortest in the middle of the day. The lower the Sun is in the sky, the longer your shadow.

You can have fun with shadows!

SEE THE SCIENCE ↴

On a sunny morning, stand a long stick in a pot of soil or sand. Use chalk to mark the stick's shadow. Repeat this every hour. Although the stick stays still, its shadow moves and changes shape. This is because the position of the **light source** (the Sun) changes.

Shadow play

A shadow is made when an object blocks the path of light. How can you change the size and shape of a shadow? **Experiment** with shadow puppets, and use what you discover to put on a show.

EQUIPMENT

- Cardboard and coloured plastic
- Scissors
- Sticks or straws
- Bright torch
- Pale, flat background or wall
- Tape measure

Method

1 Make shadow puppets by sticking cardboard characters on to straws or sticks. Light will not travel through the **opaque** card, but you can make eyes and other features by cutting holes.

Take care when using scissors and ask an adult to help you.

ADULT HELP

2   Place a torch on a table two metres from a pale wall or sheet.

3   Hold a puppet one metre from the torch. Does it cast a shadow on the wall? Measure and record the height of the shadow.

Predict: Will the shadow get bigger or smaller if you move the puppet away from the torch?

4   Move the puppet further away from the torch. How big is the shadow now?

5   Move the puppet closer to the torch. How big is the shadow now? Copy and complete the table below to record your results. This will make it easier to compare them.

Distance of object from light source (cm)	Height of shadow (cm)
100	
150	
200	
50	
20	

Conclusion

You can change the size of a shadow by changing the distance between the object and the **light source**. Moving an object closer to the light source makes its shadow larger, because it blocks more of the light from the source. Moving an object farther from the light source makes its shadow smaller, because it blocks less of the light from the source.

Try these shadow challenges.

1 Can you change the shape of a shadow by turning the object? What happens when you turn a shadow puppet side on to the wall? Measure and record the height of the shadow.

2 Add a second **light source**. Can you give an object more than one shadow?

3 Stick coloured plastic over the end of the torch to change the colour of the light source. What happens to the shadows?

4 Make shadow puppets using **translucent** and **transparent** materials. Do they cast shadows? Are the shadows different from those cast by **opaque** objects?

5 Compare the shadows cast by large and small light sources (such as a desk lamp and a torch). How are they different?

6 Put on a shadow puppet play!
Use what you've found out about shadows to put on a puppet show. Can you make the shadows of your puppets and real people the same size?

Make a screen using a sheet hung from a clothes line. Shine light behind the screen and cast shadows on the screen, so the audience only sees the shadows.

How do mirrors work?

When light hits an object, some light is absorbed. Some bounces off and changes direction. We say it has been **reflected**. Different surfaces reflect light in different ways.

Paper has a **dull** rough surface. It reflects light, but scatters it in different directions. Some of the reflected light reaches your eyes wherever you stand. Smooth shiny surfaces reflect light without scattering it.

SEE THE SCIENCE ⬇

Take care when using the mirror and torch.

Put a piece of paper on the floor. Shine a torch at the paper. Can you see a light spot where the beam hits the paper? Can you see it from different places? Replace the paper with a mirror. Shine the torch at the mirror. Can you see a light spot where the beam hits the mirror? Can you see it from anywhere in the room?

When you stand in front of a mirror, light reflected from your face bounces off the mirror and back towards your eyes without being scattered. You see an image of yourself in the mirror.

Why can't you see your reflection if you look at a mirror from the side? Rays of light hitting an object always bounce off at the same angle as they travelled towards it. Light hitting a mirror from the side will bounce off to the other side, like a ball kicked against a wall.

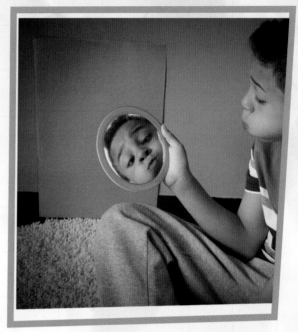

REAL WORLD SCIENCE

White light is made up of all the colours of the rainbow (see page 7). Objects look a certain colour because they reflect some of the colours and absorb the rest. This T-shirt absorbs every colour except red, and reflects only the red light to your eyes.

Goal!

Is it possible to **predict** where light will be **reflected** when it hits a mirror? Challenge yourself to a game of light football and find out.

EQUIPMENT

- Bright torch
- Black cardboard
- Scissors
- Sticky tape
- White paper
- Mirror
- Coloured pencils
- Ruler
- Protractor

Glass mirrors can be dangerous if you break them. Use plastic mirrors, or ask an adult to help you use a glass mirror.

ADULT HELP

Method

1 Stick two semi-circles of black card over the head of the torch, leaving a gap of a few millimetres in the middle.

2 Draw a football pitch on a sheet of white paper.

3 Place the paper pitch on a flat table, and set up a mirror where the red cross is in the picture. Darken the room.

Predict: Where will you need to put the torch to score a "goal" with light?

5 Use the torch to bounce a beam of light off the mirror and into the goal. Use a pencil to mark the path of the light beam before and after it hits the mirror.

5 Use a protractor to measure the angle between each line and the centre line on the pitch. Repeat step 4 to score goals from different starting points. Mark the path of each light beam before and after it hits the mirror. Use a different colour for each goal.

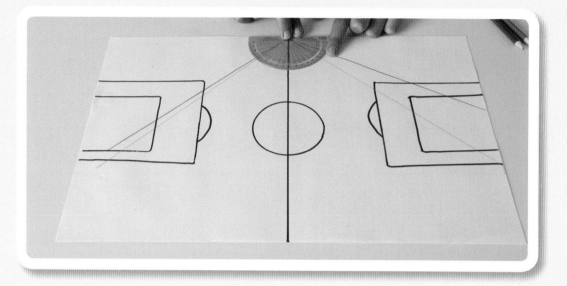

IS IT A FAIR TEST?

Make sure you only change the position of the torch each time. The position of the mirror should stay the same.

6 Copy and complete the table to record your results.

Goal	Angle between the beam of light and the centre line	Angle between reflected ray and dotted line
1		
2		
3		
4		

Can you score goals by changing the position of the mirror instead of the torch?

Conclusion

When light leaves the torch it travels in a straight line. When it hits the mirror, the light is **reflected** and travels away in a different direction. The light is reflected at exactly the same angle as it hits the mirror.

Plan your next experiment

Experiments have helped you discover some amazing things about light. Just like you, scientists carry out experiments to answer questions and test ideas. Each experiment is planned carefully to make it a fair test.

YOU ASKED...

YOU FOUND OUT THAT...

Can we see without light?

- We see **light sources** when the light they give out enters our eyes.
- We can also see objects that don't give out their own light, but only when light from a source bounces off them towards our eyes. Without light, we cannot see.

Which materials let light pass through them?

- **Transparent** materials let most light pass through them. We can see through them clearly.
- **Translucent** materials let some light pass through them.
- **Opaque** materials do not let light travel through them. A shadow forms on the far side of the object.

How do shadows change when we change the distance between an object and light source?

- We see a shadow when an object blocks the path of light.
- The closer the light source is to the object, the larger the shadow.

Can you **predict** where light will be **reflected** when it hits a mirror?

- When light bounces off an object, we say it has been reflected.
- Each light ray is reflected at the same angle as it hits the object.
- A rough surface **scatters** reflected light in different directions.
- A smooth, shiny surface bounces the light in one direction.

Experiments also lead to new questions! Did you think of more questions about light? Can you plan experiments to help answer them?

Being a scientist and carrying out experiments is exciting. What will you discover next?

> Glass mirrors can break into sharp pieces. Be careful and ask an adult to help you if you are planning an experiment using glass mirrors.

ADULT HELP

WHAT NEXT?

Do glow-in-the-dark materials reflect light or give out their own light? Plan an experiment to find out.

When light passes through a gap, does the size of the gap affect the light? Plan an experiment to find out.

Does the shadow of an object change if the light source is bigger or smaller than the object? Plan an experiment to find out.

What happens when you bounce a reflected beam of light off a second mirror? Does it change direction again? Plan an experiment to find out.

Glossary

analyse examine the results of an experiment carefully in order to explain what happened

bioluminescence when living things give off light

chemical change when different substance react together and change

dull not shiny

energy the power to make something happen

experiment procedure carried out to test an idea or answer a question

light source something that gives off energy as light

observation noting or measuring what you see, hear, smell or feel

opaque does not let light pass through

prediction best guess or estimate of what will happen, based on what you already know

reflect bounce light away without absorbing it or letting it pass through

reflected when light bounces off an object and changes direction

scatter reflect or bend light rays so they travel away in many different directions

translucent lets some light pass through, but not enough to see clearly through it

transparent lets light pass through; see-through

vacuum completely empty space

variable something that can be changed

Find out more

Books

Essential Physical Science: Light and Sound, Louise and Richard Spilsbury (Raintree, 2013)

Flash! Light and How We See Things, Peter Riley (Franklin Watts, 2012)

Science Experiments, Robert Winston (DK, 2011)

Websites

kids.britannica.com/lm/animations/ovision001d4/product.html
Find out how your eyes work.

www.bbc.co.uk/learningzone/clips/light-sources-in-your-bedroom-at-night/2428.html
Watch a video about light sources in your bedroom!

www.bbc.co.uk/schools/scienceclips/ages/7_8/light_shadows.shtml
Experiment with shadows online – no equipment needed!

www.childrensuniversity.manchester.ac.uk/interactives/science/earthandbeyond/shadows/
Experiment with sunlight and shadows without having to wait for a sunny day.

Index